Written by Sandra J Freeman
All scripture is English Standard Version
Scripture for each day and lines provided for personal reflection.

All scripture is English Standard Version
This publication contains The Holy Bible, English Standard Version, copyright © 2001, 2007, 2011, 2016 by Crossway Bibles a division of Good News Publishers. The ESV text has been reproduced in cooperation with and by permission of Good News Publishers.

With thanks to Karen Edwards for technical and formatting support.

Dedicated To my Lord and Savior who loves me fully every single day.

January

He had searched for the little house, and now at the end of a rocky path, he found it. The purchase came at great personal cost. He loved everything about the tiny cabin even though he knew there was much work to be done. First, he rebuilt the foundation making it sturdy and straight. Then, he set about restoring the hearth which had been torn down and left with no vigor of its own. Stone after stone of it was lovingly and patiently arranged so that after a season, it offered him the warmth of its glow.

With tender strokes he smoothed the rough hewn wood of the walls. He washed the floors on bended knee until they were white as snow.

The devoted little house yielded each room to his gentle care for meticulous examination. Each corner, Doorway, and closet was known to him.

Emptiness was gone from the dwelling. Joy became visible through each window. He cherished his home; and in return it became a reflection of the One who lived there.

Then, peace fell forever upon the small house. A sheltering tree stood guard over it, and a beautiful river sang a melody to it night and day.

How lovely is your dwelling place, O Lord of hosts! Psalm 84:1

Take a Moment….
….to pray for your spouse or pastor

_____

_____
_____
_____

January 1
For no matter how many promises God has made, they are "Yes" in Christ. And so through him the "Amen" is spoken by us to the glory of God. 2 Corinthians 1:20

_____
_____
_____
_____
_____
_____
_____

January 2
When you pass through the waters, I will be with you; And when you pass through the rivers, they will not sweep over you. When you walk through the fire, you will not be burned. The flames will not set you ablaze; Isaiah 43:2:

_____
_____
_____
_____
_____
_____

January 3
Consider the ravens: They do not sow or reap, they have no storeroom or barn; yet God feeds them. And how much more valuable you are then birds! Luke 12:24

_____
_____
_____
_____

January 4
He tends his flock like a shepherd: He gathers the lambs in his arms and carries them close to his heart; he gently leads those that have young. Isaiah 40:1

_____
_____
_____
_____
_____
_____
_____

January 5
The Lord is close to the brokenhearted and saves those who are crushed in spirit. Psalm 34:18

_____
_____
_____
_____
_____
_____
_____

January 6
You did not choose me, but I chose you and appointed you to go and bear fruit- fruit that will last. Then the father will give you whatever you ask in my name. John 15:16

_____
_____
_____
_____
_____
_____

January 7
You will seek me and find me when you seek me with all your heart. Jeremiah 29:13

_____
_____
_____
_____
_____
_____

Take a Moment....
....to soak in a bubble bath.

_____
_____
_____
_____
_____
_____

January 8
I always thank my God as I remember you in my prayers, because I hear about your faith in the Lord Jesus and your love for all the saints.
Philemon 1:4 & 5

_____
_____
_____
_____
_____
_____

January 9
Know that the Lord has set apart the godly for himself;
the Lord will hear when I call to him. Psalm 4:3

_____
_____
_____
_____
_____
_____

January 10
I am the good shepherd. The good shepherd lays down
his life for the sheep. John 10:11

_____
_____
_____
_____
_____
_____

January 11
Do not be deceived: God cannot be mocked. A man reaps what he sows. Galatians 6:7

_____
_____
_____
_____
_____
_____

January 12
Now faith is being sure of what we hope for and certain of what we do not see. Hebrews 11:1

_____
_____
_____
_____
_____
_____

January 13
For you did not receive a spirit that makes you a slave to fear, but you received the Spirit of Sonship. Romans 8:15

_____
_____
_____

January 14
Come to me, all you who are weary and burdened, and I will give you rest. Matthew 11:28

_____
_____
_____
_____

Quiet Moments…..

The Lord said to Moses, "Have all the people of Israel build me a holy sanctuary so I can live among them." Amazing! The creator of the universe wanted to live among quarreling, complaining people.

In the New Testament, God lived among men for 33 years, than in the ultimate act of love, gave his life so that we could be with him in eternity.

He loves us even though he sees our every thought and act, and knows every intention of our hearts.
Our God is awesome.

Take a Moment.......
.......to call a Friend

_____
_____
_____
_____
_____
_____

January 15
You, dear children, are from God and have overcome them, because the one who is in you is greater than the one who is in the world. 1 John 4:4

_____
_____
_____
_____
_____
_____

January 16
For you have been born again, not of perishable seed, but of imperishable, through the living and enduring word of God. 1 Peter 1:23

January 17
So we say with confidence, "The Lord is my helper; I will not be afraid. What can man do to me?" Hebrews 13:6

January 18
He who dwells in the shelter of the Most High will rest in the shadow of the Almighty. I will say of the Lord, "He is my refuge and my fortress, my God, in whom I trust." Psalm 97:1

_____
_____
_____
_____
_____
_____
_____

January 19
And my God will meet all your needs according to his glorious riches in Christ Jesus. Philippians 4:19

_____
_____
_____
_____
_____

January 20
...I will tell of the kindness of the Lord, the deeds for which he is to be praised, according to all the Lord has done for us. Isaiah 63:7

_____
_____
_____
_____
_____
_____

January 21
If you make the Most High your dwelling- even the Lord, who is my refuge- then no harm will befall you, no disaster will come near your tent. Psalm 91:9 & 10

_____
_____
_____
_____
_____
_____

Take a Moment….
….to enjoy your favorite movie.

_____
_____
_____
_____
_____
_____

January 22
For we are God's fellow workers; you are God's field, God's building. 1 Corinthians 3:9

_____
_____
_____
_____
_____

January 23
For just as the Father raises the dead and gives them life, even so the Son gives life to whom he is pleased to give it. John 5:21

_____
_____
_____
_____
_____
_____

January 24
But those who hope in the Lord will renew their strength. They will run and not grow weary, they will walk and not be faint. Isaiah 40:31

_____
_____
_____
_____
_____
_____

January 25
Submit yourselves, then, to God. Resist the devil, and he will flee from you. Come near to God and he will come near to you. James 4:7 & 8

_____
_____
_____
_____
_____
_____

January 26
Even though I walk through the valley of the shadow of death, I will fear no evil, for you are with me;
Psalm 23:4

_____
_____
_____
_____
_____
_____

January 27
Peacemakers who sow in peace raise a harvest of righteousness. James 3:18

January 28
The Lord is my shepherd; I shall not be in want. Psalm 23:1

Take a Moment…..
….to tell someone that you appreciate them.

_____
_____
_____
_____
_____
_____

January 29
I call to the Lord, who is worthy of praise, and I am saved from my enemies. 2 Samuel 22:4

_____
_____
_____
_____
_____
_____

January 30
For where two or three come together in my name, there am I with them. Matthew 18:20

January 31
Do not judge, and you will not be judged. Do not condemn, and you will not be condemned. Forgive, and you will be forgiven. Luke 6:37

February

I lift my face
And you are there
Coming close to hear
My heart in prayer
Your love is holding me
In your embrace
I am free
I close my eyes and
Hear your voice
Reaching my soul
Giving me a choice
Your love is inviting me
To become all you can see

February 1
Therefore, since we have been justified through faith, we have peace with God through our Lord Jesus Christ, through whom we have gained access by faith into this grace in which we now stand. And we rejoice in the hope of the glory of God. Romans 5:1 & 2

_____
_____
_____
_____
_____

February 2
Praise the Lord, O my soul; all my inmost being, praise his holy name. Psalm 103: 5

_____
_____
_____
_____
_____

February 3
Jesus said to her, "I am the resurrection and the life. He who believes in me will live, even though he dies; and whoever lives and believes in me will never die. Do you believe this?" John 11:25

_____
_____
_____
_____
_____

February 4
Let us not become weary in doing good, for at the proper time we will reap a harvest if we do not give up. Galatians 6:9

_____
_____
_____
_____
_____
_____

Take a Moment….
….to read a good book.

_____
_____
_____
_____
_____

February 5
Unless the Lord builds the house, its builders labor in vain. Unless the Lord watches over the city, the watchmen stand guard in vain. Psalm 127:1

_____
_____
_____
_____
_____
_____

February 6
And now these three remain: faith, hope and love. But the greatest of these is love. 1 Corinthians 13:13

February 7
My soul finds rest in God alone; my salvation comes from him. Psalm 62: 1

February 8
Surely the arm of the Lord is not too short to save, nor his ear too dull to hear. Isaiah 59:1

February 9
The Lord is far from the wicked but he hears the prayer of the righteous. Proverbs 15:29

February 10
The fear of the Lord leads to life: Then one rests content, untouched by trouble. Proverbs 19:23

February 11
Command them to do good, to be rich in good deeds, and to be generous and willing to share. 1 Timothy 6:18

Take a Moment….
….to write a thank you note.

_____
_____
_____
_____
_____
_____
_____

February 12
Better a meal of vegetables where there is love than a fattened calf with hatred. Proverbs 15:17

_____
_____
_____
_____
_____
_____
_____

February 13
The Lord will keep you from all harm- he will watch over your life; the Lord will watch over your coming and going both now and forevermore. Psalm 121:7

_____
_____
_____
_____
_____
_____

February 14
The Lord is good, a refuge in times of trouble. He cares for those who trust in him. Nahum 1:7

_____
_____
_____
_____
_____
_____

Quiet moments......

Everything in Eve's world was beautiful and perfect. She came face to face with evil and didn't recognize it. When satan spoke to her, she had no reason to be afraid. As Christians we can choose to concentrate on good things and pretend that evil doesn't exist. Would doing that have solved Eve's problem? Why should we think about this? The church body often tells us to be happy and at peace. We often feel as though we should ignore evil. Satan hates God's image bearers. His intent is to corrupt humanity. What should Eve have done that day in the Garden of Eden? She should have said, "Let me talk to God about this". But, she didn't. She did what seemed right to her. She trusted the serpent because she didn't see evil.

Eve didn't see it coming.

The bible tells us to ask God for wisdom and to trust him. Ephesians 6:10 tells us to put on the full armor of God. Only warriors need armor. Only war needs warriors. We are warriors in God's army. We have a real enemy

February 15
I am bringing my righteousness near, it is not far away; and my salvation will not be delayed. Isaiah 46:13

February 16
Jesus Christ is the same yesterday and today and forever. Hebrews 13:8

February 17
Do not boast about tomorrow, for you do not know what a day may bring forth. Proverbs 27:1

_____
_____
_____
_____
_____
_____

February 18
If you remain in me and my words remain in you, ask whatever you wish, and it will be given you.
John 15:7

_____
_____
_____
_____
_____
_____

Take a Moment….
…to take a walk.

February 19
The angel of the Lord encamps around those who fear him, and he delivers them. Psalm 34:7

February 20
"If you can?" said Jesus. "Everything is possible for him who believes." Mark 9:23

February 21
But the needy will not always be forgotten, nor the hope of the afflicted ever perish. Psalm 9:18

February 22
In him and through faith in him we may approach God with freedom and confidence. Ephesians 3:12

_____
_____
_____
_____
_____
_____

February 23
"For I will forgive their wickedness and will remember their sins no more" Hebrews 8:12

_____
_____
_____
_____
_____
_____

February 24
But I, with a song of thanksgiving, will sacrifice to you. What I have vowed I will make good. Salvation comes from the Lord. Jonah 2:9

February 25
If you, then, though you are evil, know how to give good gifts to your children, how much more will your Father in heaven give good gifts to those who ask him! Matthew 7:11

Take a Moment….
….to pray for your pastor.

February 26
Therefore confess your sins to each other and pray for each other so that you may be healed. The prayer of a righteous man is powerful and effective. James 5:16

February 27
Delight yourself in the Lord and he will give you the desires of your heart. Psalm 37:4

_____
_____
_____
_____
_____
_____

February 28
But seek ye first the kingdom of God, and his righteousness, and all these things will be given to you as well. Matthew 6:33

_____
_____
_____
_____
_____
_____

February 29
He will cover you with his feathers, and under his wings you will find refuge; his faithfulness will be your shield and rampart. Psalm 91:4

March

God sends His angels
To keep you safe
They guide you lovingly
Along the way
God's eye is upon you
And His wisdom directs you
God's strength helps you to endure
His arm holds you to give you comfort
May His peace be upon you
As He directs your path today

March 1
The name of the Lord is a fortified tower; the righteous run into it and are safe. Proverbs 18:10

_____
_____
_____
_____
_____
_____

March 2
My prayer is not that you take them out of the world, but that you protect them from the evil one. John 17:15

_____
_____
_____
_____
_____
_____

March 3
A cheerful heart is good medicine, but a crushed spirit dries up the bones. Proverbs 17:22

Take a Moment....
....to memorize a scripture.

March 4
Lazy hands make a man poor, but diligent hands bring wealth. Proverbs 10:4

_____
_____
_____
_____
_____
_____

March 5
Jesus answered, " I am the way, and the truth, and the life. No one comes to the Father, except through me." John 14:6

_____
_____
_____
_____
_____
_____

March 6
This is the confidence we have in approaching God: that, if we ask anything according to His will, He hears us.
1 John 5:14

March 7
This is the day the Lord has made; let us rejoice and be glad in it. Psalm 118:24

March 8
Jesus Christ is the same yesterday and today and forever.
Hebrews 13:8

_____
_____
_____
_____
_____
_____

March 9
Trust in the Lord and do good; dwell in the land and enjoy safe pasture. Psalm 37:3

_____
_____
_____
_____
_____
_____

Take a Moment….
….to give someone a hug.

_____
_____
_____
_____
_____
_____

March 10
"I am the true vine, and my Father is the gardener. He cuts off every branch in me that bears no fruit, while every branch that does bear fruit he prunes so that it will be even more fruitful. John 15:1& 2

_____
_____
_____
_____
_____
_____

March 11
Rejoice in the Lord always. I will say it again: Rejoice!
Philippians 4:4

March 12
Peace I leave with you; my peace I give you. I do not give to you as the world gives. Do not let your hearts be troubled and do not be afraid. John 14:27

March 13
Therefore I tell you, whatever you ask for in prayer, believe that you have received it, and it will be yours.
Mark 11:24

March 14
The Lord is my rock, my fortress, and my deliverer; my God is my rock, in whom I take refuge, my shield, and the horn of my salvation. He is my stronghold, my refuge, my savior- from violent men you save me. 2 Samuel 22:2& 3

Quiet moments…..

I see the lack in my life when I look around to see what others have got.

I become inadequate when I focus on persons who seem to have quite a lot.

My talents don't measure up to the gifted people I see.

I am never enough, Lord, when my view reaches toward others or stops at me

Please keep my eyes on you, Father.
Your grace is sufficient until…Comparisons make me too less
And keep me from doing your will.

March 15
Blessed are those who are persecuted because of righteousness, for theirs is the kingdom of heaven.
Matthew 5:10

March 16
"I am the Lord, the God of all mankind. Is anything too hard for me?" Jeremiah 32:27

March 17
For God so loved the world, that He gave his one and only Son, that whoever believes in him shall not perish but have eternal life. John 3:16

Take A Moment….
…..to pray for an unsaved friend.

March 18
My soul finds rest in God alone; my salvation comes from him. He alone is my rock and my salvation; he is my fortress, I will never be shaken. Psalm 62:1& 2

March 19
Blessed are the peacemakers: for they will be called sons of God. Matthew 5:9

March 20
Let us hold unswervingly to the hope we profess, for he who promised is faithful. Hebrews 10:23

_____
_____
_____
_____
_____
_____
_____

March 21
"I am coming soon. Hold on to what you have, so that no one will take your crown." Revelation 3:11

_____
_____
_____
_____
_____
_____
_____

March 22
With God we will gain the victory, and he will trample down our enemies. Psalm 60:12

_____
_____
_____
_____
_____
_____

March 23
Blessed are the merciful, for they will be shown mercy. Blessed are the pure in heart, for they will see God. Matthew 5:7& 8

_____
_____
_____
_____
_____

March 24
Know that the Lord is God. It is he who made us, and we are his; we are his people, and the sheep of his pasture.
Psalm 100:3

Take a Moment....
... to go for a drive in the country.

March 25
Blessed are the meek: for they shall inherit the earth.
Matthew 5:5

_____
_____
_____
_____
_____
_____

March 26
It is more blessed to give than to receive. Acts 20:35

_____
_____
_____
_____
_____
_____

March 27
It was good for me to be afflicted so that I might learn your decrees. The law from your mouth is more precious to me than thousands of pieces of silver and gold.
Psalm 119:71& 72

_____
_____
_____
_____
_____
_____

March 28
When Christ, who is your life, appears, then you also will appear with Him in glory. Colossians 3:4

_____
_____
_____
_____
_____
_____

March 29
There is no one holy like the Lord: for there is no one besides you; there is no Rock like our God.
1 Samuel 2:2

March 30
So do not fear, for I am with you; do not be dismayed, for I am your God. I will strengthen you and help you; I will uphold you with my righteous right hand.
Isaiah 41: 10

March 31
Blessed is the one you discipline, Lord, the one you teach from your law; Psalm 94:12

_____
_____
_____
_____
_____
_____

Take a Moment….
….to treat a friend to lunch.

_____
_____
_____
_____
_____
_____

<u>April</u>

Your heart reaches up toward God
And He sees your beautiful face
As He touches your soul with strength
And comfort, you know that you belong to Him
He loves you more than any person ever will
It is this knowledge spoken over and over
Into your life that causes you to reach out to others
You long for them to feel that beloved caress that
Heals the soul and brings the beauty of peace

April 1
Peace I leave with you; my peace I give to you; I do not give to you as the world gives. Do not let your hearts be troubled and do not be afraid. John 14:27

_____
_____
_____
_____
_____

April 2
There is a way which seems right to a man, but in the end it leads to death. Proverbs 14:12

_____
_____
_____
_____
_____

April 3
Worship the Lord your God; it is he who will deliver you from he hand of all your enemies. 2 Kings 17:39

_____
_____
_____
_____
_____
_____

April 4
Charm is deceptive, and beauty is fleeting; but a woman who fears the Lord is to be praised. Proverbs 31:30

_____
_____
_____
_____
_____
_____

April 5
But the Lord is faithful, and he will strengthen you and protect you from the evil one. 2 Thessalonians 3:3

April 6
Now the Lord is the Spirit, and where the Spirit of the Lord is, there is freedom. 2 Corinthians 3:17

April 7
But our citizenship is in heaven. And we eagerly await a Savior from there, the Lord Jesus Christ.
Philippians 3:20

Take a Moment….
…to plan a fun weekend.

April 8
But he gives us more grace. That is why scripture says: "God opposes the proud but shows favor to the humble". James 4:6

_____
_____
_____
_____
_____
_____

April 9
My flesh and my heart may fail, but God is the strength of my heart and my portion forever. Psalm 73:26

_____
_____
_____
_____
_____
_____

April 10
The world and its desires pass away, but whoever does the will of God lives forever. 1 John 2:17

April 11
Praise be to the Lord, to God our Savior, who daily bears our burdens. Our God is a God who saves;
Psalm 68:19& 20

April 12
I have come into the world as a light, so that no one who believes in me should stay in darkness. John 12:46

April 13
If you believe, you will receive whatever you ask for in prayer. Matthew 21:22

April 14
Commit to the Lord whatever you do, and your plans will succeed. Proverbs 16:3

Take a Moment….
…to invite someone to church.

Quiet moments....

Jesus took his closest friends with him everywhere he went. Daily he taught them, laughed with them, and touched their lives. They went where he went, ate what he ate, and saw his loving kindness every day. They were privileged to hear his parables and witness his miracles firsthand. Jesus loved each man. One night, Jesus was betrayed by two of the men that he had called, 'friend.' Their names were Judas and Peter. After Jesus had been arrested, beaten, and sentenced to death; both men regretted their betrayal. Judas took his own sin upon his back, and hung himself because the weight of it was more than he could bear. Peter was ashamed for what he had done, but believed that Jesus was the Son of God. He gave the weight of his sin to Jesus. He loved and trusted him.

Jesus had loved both Judas and Peter. He had given his life for both men. Judas refused to accept the gift that had been freely given. Peter went on to live his life for Jesus.

Sea of Galilee

April 15
For the Lord watches over the way of the righteous, but the way of the wicked will perish. Psalm 1:6

April 16
He who has the Son has life; he who does not have the Son of God does not have life. 1 John 5:12

April 17
The Lord redeems his servants; no one will be condemned who takes refuge in him. Psalm 34:22

April 18
This is love: not that we loved God, but that he loved us, and sent his Son as an atoning sacrifice for our sins.
1 John 4:10

April 19
For the Son of man came to seek and to save what was lost. Luke 19:10

April 20
From heaven the Lord looks down and sees all mankind; from his dwelling place he watches all who live on earth- he who forms the hearts of all, who considers everything they do. Psalm 33:13-15

April 21
There is a time for everything, and a season for every activity under heaven. Ecclesiastes 3:1

_____
_____
_____
_____
_____

Take a Moment….
,,,,to learn a new praise song.

_____
_____
_____
_____
_____

April 22
It is good to praise the Lord, and make music to your name, O most High, to proclaim your love in the morning and your faithfulness at night, Psalm 92:1& 2

April 23
As the Scripture says, "Anyone who trusts in him will never be put to shame." Romans 10:11

April 24
I tell you the truth, anyone who will not receive the kingdom of God like a little child will never enter it.
Mark 10:15

_____
_____
_____
_____
_____
_____

April 25
For whoever does the will of my Father in heaven is my brother and sister and mother. Matthew 12:50

_____
_____
_____
_____
_____
_____

April 26
"See, I will create new heavens and a new earth. The former things will not be remembered, nor will they come to mind." Isaiah 65:17

_____
_____
_____
_____
_____
_____

April 27
Blessed are those who hunger and thirst for righteousness: for they will be filled. Matthew 5:6

_____
_____
_____
_____
_____
_____

April 28
The thief comes only to steal and kill and destroy; I have come that they may have life, and have it to the full. John 10:10

___

Take a Moment….
….to visit the elderly.

___

April 29
Cast your cares on the Lord and he will sustain you: he will never let the righteous fall. Psalm 55:22

April 30
The fear of the Lord is the beginning of knowledge, but fools despise wisdom and discipline. Proverbs 1:7

May

Into every life a little rain must fall
It is this rain that causes the flower of your life
To grow and blossom into beauty
Always remember that you are
Never alone
It is God who gives you strength to endure
Because He loves you very much
And His plan is for you to grow

1 Peter 2:24 He himself bore our sins in his body on the tree, that we might die to sin and live to righteousness. By His wounds you have been healed.

May 1
So you are no longer a slave, but a son; and since you are a son:, God has made you also an heir.. Galatians 4:7

May 2
Therefore, if anyone is in Christ, he is a new creation; the old has gone, the new has come! 2 Corinthians 5:17

May 3
For this God is our God for ever and ever; he will be our guide even to the end. Psalm 48:14

May 4
And in him you too are being built together to become a dwelling in which God lives by his Spirit. Ephesians 2:22

May 5
This is how we know what love is: Jesus Christ laid down his life for us. 1 John 3:16

_____
_____
_____
_____
_____
_____

Take a Moment…...
…….to enjoy a garden

_____
_____
_____
_____
_____
_____

May 6
God is our refuge and strength, an ever-present help in trouble. Psalm 46:1

May 7
The fruit of the righteous is a tree of life, and he that wins souls is wise. Proverbs 11:30

May 8
Cast all your anxiety on him because he cares for you.
1 Peter 5:7

May 9
Blessed are the poor in spirit, for theirs is the kingdom of heaven. Matthew 5:3

May 10
The Lord will guide you always; he will satisfy your needs in a sun-scorched land and will strengthen your frame. Isaiah 58:11

May 11
I can do everything through him who gives me strength. Philippians 4:13

May 12

The Lord is near to all who call on him, to all who call on Him in truth. He fulfills the desires of those who fear him; Psalm 145:18& 19

_____
_____
_____
_____
_____
_____

Happy Mother's Day

Take a Moment…..
….to bake a pie for a friend or neighbor.

_____
_____
_____
_____
_____
_____

May 13
The Lord is gracious and compassionate, slow to anger and rich in love. The Lord is good to all; he has compassion on all he has made. Psalm 145:8& 9

_____
_____
_____
_____
_____
_____

May 14
God is not unjust; he will not forget your work and the love you have shown him as you helped his people and continue to help them. Hebrews 6:10

_____
_____
_____
_____
_____
_____

Quiet moments…

Today, Lord I felt your presence as you came to my door
and knocked. I saw the joy in your eyes when I opened
my heart to you
As you came in and I told you all that I felt, good and
bad,
I saw no condemnation on your kind face. You accepted
me just as I am
Then my soul delighted in you
I rested because your love enveloped me
My sin was forgiven and I was set free.
You gave me peace that I could never fully understand.

I love you, Lord, because you first loved me

May 15
The Lord our God is merciful and forgiving, even though we have rebelled against Him. Daniel 9:9

May 16
The Lord is righteous in all His ways and loving toward all he has made. The Lord is near to all who call on him, Psalm 145:17& 18

May 17
Jesus answered, "It is written: Man does not live on bread alone, but on every word that comes from the mouth of God." Matthew 4:4

May 18
I will lie down and sleep in peace, for you alone, O Lord, make me dwell in safety.. Psalm 4:8

May 19
If you are insulted because of the name of Christ, you are blessed, for the Spirit of glory and of God rests on you. 1 Peter 4:14

Take a Moment....
.....to enjoy a play.

May 20
But God demonstrates his own love for us in this: While we were still sinners, Christ died for us. Romans 5:8

May 21
Though I walk in the midst of trouble, you preserve my life; you stretch out your hand against the anger of my foes, with your right hand you save me. Psalm 138:7

May 22
Then he said to them all: "If anyone would come after me, he must deny himself and take up his cross daily and follow me." Luke 9:23

_____
_____
_____
_____
_____
_____

May 23
He gives strength to the weary and increases the power of the weak. Isaiah 40:29

_____
_____
_____
_____
_____
_____

May 24
If we are faithless, he will remain faithful: for he cannot disown himself. 2 Timothy 2:13

May 25
Each man should give what he has decided in his heart to give, not reluctantly or under compulsion, for God loves a c cheerful giver. 2 Corinthians 9:7

May 26
He is like a tree planted by streams of water, which yields its fruit in season and whose leaf does not wither. Whatever he does prospers. Psalm 1:3

Take a Moment....
....to read a story to a child.

May 27
I write to you, dear children, because your sins have been forgiven on account of his name. 1 John 2:12

May 28
But I tell you: "Love your enemies and pray for those who persecute you, that you may be sons of your Father in heaven." Matthew 5:44

May 29
The Lord will fulfill his purpose, for me; your love, O Lord, endures forever- do not abandon the works of your hands. Psalm 138:8

_____
_____
_____
_____
_____
_____

May 30
Therefore we do not lose heart. Though outwardly we are wasting away, yet inwardly we are being renewed day by day. 2 Corinthians 4:16

_____
_____
_____
_____
_____
_____

May 31
A father to the fatherless, a defender of widows, is God in his holy dwelling. Psalm 68:5

Greater love has no one than this, that someone lay down his life for his friends.
John 15:13

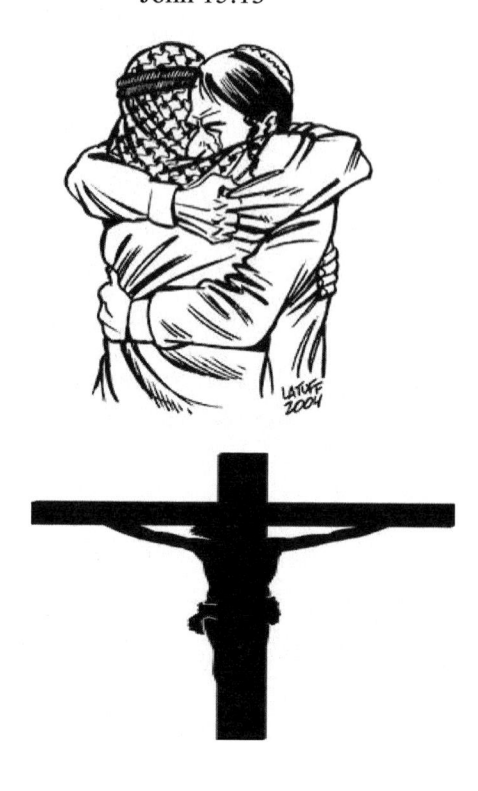

June

God bless you today and every day
May you feel His hand upon your shoulder
Gently guiding you in all that you do
And, every time your heart is afraid, anxious,
Or hurt for even a second
May you close your eyes and hear
His heart beating, giving you life,
Reassurance, and hope

June 1

If we confess our sins, he is faithful and just and will forgive us our sins and purify us from all unrighteousness. 1 John 1:9

_____
_____
_____
_____

June 2

For God did not give us a spirit of timidity, but a spirit of power, of love, and of self-discipline. 2 Timothy 1:7

_____
_____
_____
_____
_____
_____
_____

Take a Moment….
….to try something new.

_____
_____
_____
_____
_____
_____
_____

June 3
But thanks be to God! He gives us the victory through our Lord Jesus Christ. 1 Corinthians 15:57

_____
_____
_____
_____
_____
_____
_____

June 4
I have put my words in your mouth and covered you with the shadow of my hand- I who set the heavens in place, who laid the foundations of the earth, and who say to Zion, 'you are my people.' Isaiah 51:16

June 5
For to me, to live is Christ and to die is gain. Philippians 1:21

June 6
I write these things to you who believe in the name of the Son of God so that you may know that you have eternal life. 1 John 5:13

June 7
He will respond to the prayer of the destitute, he will not despise their plea. Psalm 102:17

June 8
But you are a chosen people, a royal priesthood, a holy nation, a people belonging to God, that you may declare the praises of him who called you out of darkness into His wonderful light. 1 Peter 2:9

June 9
If you obey my commands, you will remain in my love, just as I have obeyed my Father's commands and remain in his love. John 15:10

Take a Moment….
….to talk to God each day.

_____
_____
_____
_____
_____
_____

June 10
A faithful man will be richly blessed, but one eager to get rich will not go unpunished. Proverbs 28:20

_____
_____
_____
_____
_____
_____

June 11
"Your throne, O God, will last forever and ever, and righteousness will be the scepter of your kingdom."
Hebrews 1:8

June 12
For the Lord is good and his love endures forever; his faithfulness continues through all generations.
 Psalm 100:5

June 13
…by one sacrifice he has made perfect forever those who are being made holy. Hebrews 10:14

June 14
But the fruit of the Spirit is love, joy, peace, patience, kindness, goodness, faithfulness, gentleness and self-control. Against such things there is no law.
Galatians 5:22& 23

Quiet Moments....

Heavenly Father,
I've had anger in my heart lately. I am angry at the injustices that someone has dealt to me.
There's part of me, Lord that wants to rail and shout, and let that person know exactly how I feel.
And, then I remember that you offer forgiveness for all of my injustices toward others.
I remember that for me to express myself with anger at anyone is a sin that will stand between you and me.
And, I know that ultimately, the reason that I want to tell a person how they have hurt me is because I don't trust you to love me enough to let them know.
I remember that no healing ever comes with angry words. And, change, whether it be in me or another, will only come because you have been there with grace and mercy reaching out with love.

I am the way and the truth and the life. No one comes to the Father except through me. John 14:6

June 15
Trust in the Lord with all your heart and lean not on your own understanding; in all your ways acknowledge him, and he will make your paths straight.
Proverbs 3:5& 6

June 16
Have I not commanded you? "Be strong and courageous. Do not be afraid; do not be discouraged, for the Lord your God will be with you wherever you go." Joshua 1:9

Take a Moment....
....send a thank-you note

_____
_____
_____
_____
_____

Happy Father's Day

June 17
For this reason Christ is the mediator of a new covenant, that those who are called may receive the promised eternal inheritance-now that he has died as a ransom to set them free from the sins committed under the first covenant. Hebrews 9:15

_____
_____
_____
_____

June 18
And God shall wipe away all tears from their eyes; and there shall be no more death, neither sorrow, nor crying, neither shall there be any more pain: for the former things are passed away. Revelations 21:4

June 19
If the Son therefore shall make you free, ye shall be free indeed. John 8:36

June 20
Blessed are those who mourn, for they will be comforted.
Matthew 5:4

June 21
You are my hiding place; you will protect me from trouble and surround me with songs of deliverance.
Psalm 32:7

June 22
All the prophets testify about him that everyone who believes in him receives forgiveness of sins through his name. Acts 10:43

June 23
Therefore, there is now no condemnation for those who are in Christ Jesus, because through Christ Jesus the law of the Spirit of life set me free from the law of sin and death. Romans 8:1

Take a Moment....
....to invite a friend to dinner.

_____
_____
_____
_____
_____

June 24
Those who know your name will trust in you, for you, Lord, have never forsaken those who seek you
Psalm 9:10

_____
_____
_____
_____
_____

June 25
For the wages of sin is death, but the free gift of God is eternal life in Christ Jesus our Lord. Romans 6:23

June 26
Your word, O Lord, is eternal; it stands firm in the heavens. Your faithfulness continues through all generations; Psalm 119:89& 90

June 27
Then Jesus declared, "I am the bread of life. He who comes to me will never go hungry, and he who believes in me will never be thirsty." John 6:35

June 28
Blessed are the pure in heart, for they will see God. Matthew 5:8

June 29
A gentle answer turns away wrath, but a harsh word stirs up anger. Proverbs 15:1

June 30
Heaven and earth will pass away, but my words will never pass away. Matthews 24:35

July

Sometimes when I wake at night
My thoughts turn to you

So, I lift you up to God
As I love to do

Knowing that God cares for you
Gives me rest

Peace and joy are mine
When you'll be blessed!

Take a Moment....
....to offer to babysit.

July 1
Dear friends, now we are children of God, and what we will be has not yet been make known. But we know that when he appears, we shall be like him, for we shall see him as he is. 1 John 3:2

July 2
"I tell you the truth, if anyone says to this mountain, 'Go, throw yourself into the sea,' and does not doubt in his heart but believes that what he says will happen, it will be done for him." Mark 11:23

_____
_____
_____
_____
_____
_____

July 3
Create in me a pure heart, O God, and renew a steadfast spirit within me. Psalm 51:10

_____
_____
_____
_____
_____
_____

July 4
How great is the love the Father has lavished on us, that we should be called children of God! 1 John 3:1

_____
_____
_____
_____
_____
_____

July 5
For the Lord loves the just and will not forsake his faithful ones. They will be protected forever.
Psalm 37:28

_____
_____
_____
_____
_____
_____

July 6
Endure hardship as discipline; God is treating you as sons. For what son is not disciplined by his father?
Hebrews 12:7

July 7
For the Lord your God is the one who goes with you to fight for you against your enemies to give you victory.
Deuteronomy 20:4

Take a Moment....

....to donate your unused clothing to charity.

___

July 8

Give, and it will be given to you. A good measure, pressed down, shaken together and running over, will be poured into your lap. For with the measure you use, it will be measured to you. Luke 6:38

July 9
Pride goes before destruction, a haughty spirit before a fall. Proverbs 16:18

July 10
That if you confess with your mouth, "Jesus is Lord," and believe in your heart that God raised him from the dead, you will be saved. Romans 10:9

July 11
How good and pleasant it is when brothers live together in unity! Psalm 135:1

July 12
"Blessed is the man whom God corrects: so do not despise the discipline of the Almighty." Job 5:17

July 13
Because he himself suffered when he was tempted, he is able to help those who are being tempted. Hebrews 2:18

July 14
You will keep in perfect peace him whose mind is steadfast, because he trusts in you. Isaiah 26:3

Quiet moments...

Love could not be imagined
My strength existed only in what others could see
Fear was carefully hidden beneath the cellar of my fortress
When pain flashed into my eyes or shook my voice,
Dread would pull it back down before it could be understood
My walls were impenetrable, and I thought I was secure.

Then, I realized that Jesus was reaching out for me
He saw my cringing heart and didn't look away
He gently broke through the glass barrier that imprisoned me
He was my peace in the war that raged against me
Jesus became my reason for survival when I heard Him whisper that I had been worth dying for

Take a Moment…
….to pray for your family.

_____
_____
_____
_____
_____
_____

July 15
If any of you lacks wisdom, he should ask God, who gives generously to all without finding fault, and it will be given to him. James 1:5

_____
_____
_____
_____
_____

July 16
Above all else, guard your heart, for it is the wellspring of life. Proverbs 4:23

_____
_____
_____
_____
_____
_____

July 17
The precepts of the Lord are right, giving joy to the heart. The commands of the Lord are radiant, giving light to the eyes. Psalm 19:8

_____
_____
_____
_____
_____
_____

July 18
But even if you should suffer for what is right, you are blessed. Do not fear what they fear; do not be frightened. 1 Peter 3:14

July 19
I say to myself, "The Lord is my portion; therefore I will wait for him." Lamentations 3:2

July 20
Remember this: Whoever sows sparingly will also reap sparingly, and whoever sows generously will also reap generously. 2 Corinthians 9:6

July 21
Then you will go on your way in safety, and your foot will not stumble; when you lie down, you will not be afraid; when you lie down, your sleep will be sweet. Proverbs 3:23 & 24

Take a Moment….
….to make a new friend.

_____
_____
_____
_____
_____

July 22
"This is the covenant I will make with the house of Israel after that time", declares the Lord. "I will put my law in their minds and write it on their hearts. I will be their God and they will be my people." Jeremiah 31:33

_____
_____
_____
_____
_____
_____

July 23
For as high as the heavens are above the earth, so great is his love for those who fear Him; as far as the east is from the west, so far has he removed our transgressions from us. Psalm 103:11 & 12

July 24
And without faith it is impossible to please God, because anyone who comes to him must believe that he exists and that he rewards those who earnestly seek him.
Hebrews 11:6

July 25
Greater love has no one than this, that he lay down his life for his friends. John 15:13

July 26
Therefore, whoever humbles himself like this child is the greatest in the kingdom of heaven. Matthew 18:4

July 27
On this mountain he will destroy the shroud that enfolds all peoples, the sheet that covers all nations; he will swallow up death forever. The Sovereign Lord will wipe away the tears from all faces; Isaiah 25:7& 8

July 28
"And when you stand praying, if you hold anything against anyone, forgive him, so that your Father in heaven may forgive you your sins." Mark 11:25

Take a Moment…..
….to visit someone that you haven't seen in awhile.

_____
_____
_____
_____
_____

July 29
You, O Lord, keep my lamp burning; my God turns my darkness into light. Psalm 18:28

_____
_____
_____
_____
_____

July 30
And we know that in all things God works for the good of those who love him, who have been called according to His purpose. Romans 8:28

_____
_____
_____
_____
_____
_____

July 31
"Honor your father and mother"-which is the first commandment with a promise- "that it may go well with you and that you may enjoy long life on the earth." Ephesians 6: 2 & 3

_____
_____
_____
_____
_____

August

Water often forces a change
Where ever it touches
Water moves deep and powerfully at times
Then becomes shallow and bubbly giving a song
As it glides along
A river meanders through mountain passes,
At times, cascading onto
Rocks below
It drifts under bridges, through forests
Sometimes becoming a stream
Small and unnoticeable
Never resting, giving life where ever it flows
Water springs from the hand of God
In the end, it returns to the hand of God
Help me, Lord, to accept the life you give
Quench my thirsty soul as I follow the path you impart to
me

When you pass through the waters, I will be with you; and when you pass through the rivers, they will not sweep over you. When you walk through the fire, you will not be burned; the flames will not set you ablaze.
Isaiah 43:2

August 1
The Lord is my rock, my fortress, and my deliverer; my God is my rock, in whom I take refuge. He is my shield and the horn of my salvation, my stronghold. Psalm 18:2

August 2
For in the gospel a righteousness from God is revealed, a righteousness that is by faith from first to last, just as it is written: "The righteous will live by faith."
Romans 1:17

August 3
Dear friends, let us love one another, for love comes from God. Everyone who loves has been born of God, and knows God. 1 John 4:7

August 4
For in Christ all the fullness of the Deity lives in bodily form. Colossians 2:9

Take a Moment....
....to visit a museum.

August 5
I am not ashamed of the gospel, because it is the power of God for the salvation of everyone who believes: first for the Jew, then for the gentile. Romans 1:16

August 6
I will pour out my Spirit on all people. Your sons and daughters will prophesy, your old men will dream dreams, your young men will see visions: Joel 2:28

August 7
God made him who had no sin to be sin for us, so that in him we might become the righteousness of God. 2 Corinthians 5:21

August 8
But godliness with contentment is great gain. For we brought nothing into the world, and we can take nothing out of it. 1Timothy 6:6

August 9
You are the salt of the earth. But if the salt loses its saltiness, how can it be made salty again? It is no longer good for anything, except to be thrown out and trampled underfoot. Matthew5:13

August 10
Whatever you do, work at it with all your heart, as working for the Lord, not men, since you know that you will receive an inheritance from the Lord as a reward. It is the Lord Christ you are serving. Colossians 3:23 & 24

August 11
Rejoice in the Lord and be glad, you righteous; sing, all you who are upright in heart! Psalm 32:11

Take a Moment….
….to send a card, email, or make a call.

_____
_____
_____
_____
_____
_____

August 12
He who conceals his sins does not prosper, but whoever confesses and renounces them finds mercy. Proverbs 28:13

_____
_____
_____
_____
_____
_____

August 13
Fight the good fight of the faith. Take hold of the eternal life to which you were called when you made your good confession. 1Timothy 6:12

August 14
If my people, who are called by my name, will humble themselves and pray and seek my face and turn from their wicked ways, then will I hear from heaven and will forgive their sin and will heal their land.
2 Chronicles 7:14

Quiet Moments…..

We have all felt fear at one time or another. Fear can be described as reverence in the presence of God. Or it can mean to be scared. Our world is fast becoming a scary place to live in some areas. God gives us answers for our fear in several verses. Isaiah 35:4 tells us to "Be strong, do not fear; your God will come, he will come with vengeance; with divine retribution he will come to save you."

John 14:27 Peace I leave with you; my peace I give you. I do not give peace to you as the world gives. Do not let your hearts be troubled and do not be afraid.

Matthew 6:34 tells us "Therefore do not worry about tomorrow, for tomorrow will worry about itself. Each day has enough trouble of its own."

But, what if you aren't saved? What if bad things happen to you or someone you love and it seems like God wasn't there? Does that mean that God has fallen off his throne? Does that mean he doesn't love me or that other person? I don't have all the answers, but I know the One who does. God sent his only Son to die because he loved us. God is in control, but sin came into the world through Adam and Eve. Sin brings much sorrow with it. The closer we walk to sin, the more open we are to the problems sin creates. As a child of God, I know that I can trust him in all circumstances. We tend to blame God when bad things happen, but we don't see how often he has pulled us (or our loved one) out of danger's reach. Sometimes, we put ourselves in bad situations and suffer because we need to learn to ask God for direction *before* stepping out.

Of course, there are also persons who don't hear or heed God's warnings. And, at times, his answer is not what we wanted it to be.

This I know, our scary world will be a safer place for us when we trust God's word in every situation.
We need to pray for our loved ones daily, depending on God's loving care in their lives.

August 15
As the Father has loved me, so have I loved you. Now remain in my love. John 15:9

August 16
And receive from him anything we ask, because we obey his commands and do what pleases him. 1 John 3:22

August 17
I, even I, am he who blots out your transgressions, for my own sake, and remembers your sins no more.
Isaiah 43:25

August 18
Not everyone who says to me, 'Lord, Lord', will enter the kingdom of heaven, but only he who does the will of my Father who is in heaven. Matthew 7:21

Take a Moment….
….to give yourself a manicure.

_____
_____
_____
_____
_____
_____

August 19
A heart at peace gives life to the body, but envy rots the bones. Proverbs 14:30

_____
_____
_____
_____
_____
_____

August 20
Do not be afraid, little flock, for your Father has been pleased to give you the kingdom. Luke 12:32

August 21
But when the time had fully come, God sent his Son, born of a woman, born under law, to redeem those under law, that we might receive the full rights of sons. Galatians 4:4 & 5

August 22
His divine power has given us everything we need for life and godliness through our knowledge of him who called us by his own glory and goodness. 2 Peter 1:3

_____
_____
_____
_____
_____
_____

August 23
The Lord gives sight to the blind, the Lord lifts up those who are bowed down, the Lord loves the righteous: Psalm 146:8

_____
_____
_____
_____
_____
_____

August 24
Here I am! I stand at the door and knock. If anyone hears my voice and opens the door, I will come in and eat with him, and he with me. Revelation 3:20

_____
_____
_____
_____
_____
_____

August 25
The eternal God is your refuge, and underneath are the everlasting arms: Deuteronomy 33:27

_____
_____
_____
_____
_____

Take a Moment……
….to spend extra time in God's presence

August 26
I will not leave you as orphans; I will come to you.
John 14:18

August 27
There is neither Jew nor Greek, slave nor free, male nor female, for you are all one in Christ Jesus.
Galatians 3:28

_____
_____
_____
_____
_____
_____
_____

August 28
The Lord will rescue me from every evil attack and will bring me safely to his heavenly kingdom. 2 Timothy 4:18

_____
_____
_____
_____
_____
_____
_____

August 29
"Don't you see that whatever enters the mouth goes into the stomach and then out of the body? But the things that come out of the mouth come from the heart, and these make a man unclean." Matthew 15:17 & 18

August 30
Don't you know that you yourselves are God's temple and that God's Spirit lives in you? 1 Corinthians 3:16

September

God's grace is more excellent
Than anything else I see
Because if it were not for grace
I would cease to be

Grace lifts me,
Comforts me, and
Gives me rest

This gift of God is given
To the lowly so we
Can become His best

Therefore, confess your sins to one another and pray for one another, that you may be healed.
James 1:5

September 1
Consequently, you are no longer foreigners and aliens, but fellow citizens with God's people and members of God's household. Ephesians 2:19

_____
_____
_____
_____
_____
_____

Take a Moment….
…to.tell someone what you like best about them.

_____
_____
_____
_____
_____
_____

September 2
The Lord is my light and my salvation-whom shall I fear? Psalm 27:1

September 3
For I am the Lord, your God, who takes hold of your right hand, and says to you, Do not fear; I will help you. Isaiah 41:13

September 4

Blessed is he who has regard for the weak; the Lord delivers him in times of trouble. Psalm 41:1

_____
_____
_____
_____
_____
_____

September 5

Therefore we do not lose heart. Though outwardly we are wasting away, yet inwardly we are being renewed day by day. For our light and momentary troubles are achieving for us an eternal glory that far outweighs them all. So we fix our eyes not on what is seen, but on what is unseen. 2 Corinthians 4:16-18

_____
_____
_____
_____
_____
_____

September 6
Humble yourselves, therefore, under God's mighty hand, that he may lift you up in due time. Cast all your anxiety on him because he cares for you. 1 Peter 5:6& 7

September 7
For sin shall not have be your master, because you are not under the law, but under grace. Romans 6:14

September 8
But now in Christ Jesus you who once were far away have been brought near through the blood of Christ.
Ephesians 2:13

Take a Moment…
….to join a Bible study.

September 9
"Therefore I tell you, do not worry about your life, what you will eat or drink; or about your body, what you will wear. Is not life more important than food, and the body more important than clothes?" Matthew 6:25

September 10
The Lord is my shepherd, I shall not be in want. He makes me lie down in green pastures, he leads me beside the quiet waters, he restores my soul. He guides me in the paths of righteousness for his name's sake.
Psalm 23:1-3

September 11
So I say, live by the Spirit, and you will not gratify the desires of the sinful nature. Galatians 5:16

September 12
Blessed is the man who makes the Lord his trust, who does not look to the proud, to those who turn aside to false gods. Psalm 40:4

September 13
"No eye has seen, nor ear has heard, no mind has conceived what God has prepared for those who love him" 1 Corinthians 2:9

_____
_____
_____
_____
_____
_____

September 14
Then Jesus said to his disciples: "Therefore I tell you, do not worry about your life, what you will eat; or about your body, what you will wear. Life is more than food and the body more than clothes." Luke 12:22

_____
_____
_____
_____
_____
_____

Quiet moments…..

The Lord crowns the year with goodness. He makes me dwell in safety. In the night His song shall be with me. He's the lifter of my head. He is the health of my countenance, and my God. He is my father who delights in me. He causes His face to shine on me. He makes me drink of the river of His pleasures. He rewards me according to my righteousness. The Lord is my refuge. He hides me under the shadow of His wings. He is near when I call upon Him. The Lord hears me in the day of trouble.
He fulfills all my petitions. He knows the secrets of my heart.
The Lord lights my candle in the darkness. He makes my way straight. He teaches me wisdom.
The Lord is the redeemer of my soul who takes away my blindness. He washes me whiter than snow.
He sets me free. He upholds me with a free spirit. He is my rock. He girds me up for battle and helps me subdue my enemy.
 Because of God, I leap over a high wall. He makes my feet like hind's feet. He sets me up on a high place. The Lord's gentleness makes me great. He is the One with the words of eternal life. He is the Holy One of God.

"So do not fear, for I am with you; do not be
dismayed,, for I am your God"
Isaiah 4:10

September 15

The Lord is my light and my salvation-whom shall I fear? The Lord is the stronghold of my life- of whom shall I be afraid? Psalm 27:1

_____
_____
_____
_____
_____
_____

Take a Moment....
....to treat your family (or yourself) to ice cream.

_____
_____
_____
_____
_____
_____

September 16
Jesus answered, "Everyone who drinks this water will be thirsty again, but whoever drinks the water I give him will never thirst. Indeed, the water I give him will become in him a spring of water welling up to everlasting life". John 4:14

September 17
For everything that was written in the past was written to teach us, so that through endurance and the encouragement of the scriptures we might have hope. Romans 15:4

September 18
"Do not judge, or you too will be judged. For in the same way you judge others, you will be judged, and with the measure you use, it will be measured to you."
 Matthew 7:1& 2

_____
_____
_____
_____
_____
_____

September 19
"A new command I give you: Love one another. As I have loved you, so you must love one another." John 13:34

_____
_____
_____
_____
_____
_____

September 20
Therefore, since we have been justified through faith, we have peace with God through our Lord Jesus Romans 5:1

September 21
Whoever believes in the Son has eternal life, but whoever rejects the Son will not see life, for God's wrath remains on him. John 3:36

September 22
For the eyes of the Lord are on the righteous and his ears are attentive to their prayers, but the face of the Lord is against those who do evil. 1 Peter 3:12

_____
_____
_____
_____
_____
_____

Take a Moment…..
….to enjoy fall leaves.

_____
_____
_____
_____
_____
_____

September 23
Do everything without complaining or arguing, so that you may become blameless and pure, children of God without fault in a crooked and depraved generation, in which you shine like stars in the universe as you hold out the word of life- Philippians 2:14-16

September 24
Now faith is being sure of what we hope for and certain of what we do not see. Hebrews 11:1

September 25
Know therefore that the Lord your God is God; he is the faithful God, keeping his covenant of love to a thousand generations of those who love him and keep his commands. Deuteronomy 7:9

September 26
Therefore, since we have been justified through faith, we have peace with God through our Lord Jesus Christ. Romans 5:1

September 27
Consider it pure joy, my brothers, whenever you face trials of many kinds, because you know that the testing of your faith develops perseverance. James 1:2& 3

September 28
Now faith is being sure of what we hope for and certain of what we do not see. Hebrews 11:1

September 29
The law of the Lord is perfect, reviving the soul. The statutes of the Lord are trustworthy, making wise the simple. Psalm 19:7

_____
_____
_____
_____
_____
_____

Take a Moment……
….to look through your photos and remember.

_____
_____
_____
_____
_____
_____

September 30
For you were like sheep going astray, but now you have returned to the Shepherd and Overseer of your souls.
1 Peter 2:25

October

I feel like I have been walking against the wind for a
long time, Lord.
I get so tired some times.
Will rest ever be my option?
My heart aches, my soul is weary
How long, Lord?
Will I ever be free of pain and misery?
Gently the soft breeze of
Your spirit envelops me.
I feel the gale no more.
Questions lay at rest in my heart.
Peace holds me.
I embrace wonderful grace.
Your love carries me.
Sadness lets go its grip.
I am saved.

October 1
When a man's ways are pleasing to the Lord, he makes even his enemies live at peace with him. Proverbs 16:7

_____
_____
_____
_____
_____
_____

October 2
God is not a man, that he should lie, nor a son of man, that he should change his mind. Does he speak and then not act? Does he promise and not fulfill? Numbers 23:19

_____
_____
_____
_____
_____
_____

October 3
The Lord is not slow in keeping his promise, as some understand slowness. He is patient with you, not wanting anyone to perish, but everyone to come to repentance. 2 Peter 3:9

October 4
The Lord redeems his servants: no one will be condemned who takes refuge in him. Psalm 34:22

October 5
For the Lord watches over the way of the righteous, but the way of the wicked will perish. Psalm 1:6

October 6
If any of you lacks wisdom, he should ask God, who gives generously to all without finding fault, and it will be given to him. James 1:5

Take a Moment….
….to thank God.

October 7
But he was pierced for our transgressions, he was crushed for our iniquities; the punishment that brought us peace was upon him, and by his wounds we are healed.
Isaiah 53:5

October 8
Rejoice and be glad, because great is your reward in heaven, for in the same way they persecuted the prophets who were before you. Matthew 5:12

October 9
The name of the Lord is a strong tower; the righteous run to it and are safe. Proverbs 18:10

October 10
For whoever wants to save his life will lose it, but whoever loses his life for me will find it.
Matthew 16:25

October 11
Praise be to the God and Father of our Lord Jesus Christ, who has blessed us in the heavenly realms with every spiritual blessing in Christ. Ephesians 1:3

October 12
My son, do not despise the Lord's discipline and do not resent his rebuke, because the Lord disciplines those he loves, as a father the son he delights in. Proverbs 3:12

_____
_____
_____
_____
_____
_____

October 13
"I will be a Father to you, and you will be my sons and daughters," says the Lord Almighty. 2 Corinthians 6:18

_____
_____
_____
_____
_____

Take a Moment....
....to sit beside someone new at church.

October 14
A man's wisdom gives him patience; it is to his glory to overlook an offense. Proverbs 19:11

Quiet Moments…..

My bible tells me in Ephesians 4:2 to be completely humble and gentle; be patient, bearing with one another in love.
Our society seems anything but humble and gentle!
How am I to be those things when angry words are being spoken around me on every kind of social media? How can I be humble and gentle in the midst of this harsh world? Bearing with one another? To me that means being patient when I don't understand or agree in a world where shouting each other down is the norm.
First, I take my eyes, mind and heart off of what the world is doing. I need to go to the bible and see what God says. He is my source in a world that seems to have gone crazy.
The bible says that in this world there will be trouble, but Jesus has overcome the world in John 16:33.
That means that no matter what's going on,
God is aware and he has an answer.
I can be humble and gentle in *my* world, trusting God to take care of everyone and everything else. If I set my eyes on God and trust that the world around my family and friends is in God's loving hands, God will take care of what I care about.
 I can't take care of the world, but God can. Nothing that is happening is a surprise to Him. He is on His throne, He is still in control. I can trust *that* at all times. I need to remember that.

If you believe, you will receive
whatever you ask
for in prayer. Matthew 21:22

October 15

And now these three remain: faith, hope, and love. But the greatest of these is love. ! Corinthians 13:13

_____
_____
_____
_____
_____
_____

October 16

I am the Lord, and there is no other; apart from me there is no God. I will strengthen you, though you have not acknowledged me, so that from the rising of the sun to the place of its setting men may know there is none besides me. Isaiah 45:5& 6

_____
_____
_____
_____
_____
_____

October 17
Now to him who is able to do immeasurably more than all we ask or imagine, according to his power that is at work within us. Ephesians 3:20

October 18
But in keeping with his promise we are looking forward to a new heaven and a new earth, 2 Peter 3:13

October 19
Whoever welcomes one of these little children in my name welcomes me; and whoever welcomes me does not welcome me but the one who sent me. Mark 9:37

October 20
Just as man is destined to die once, and after that to face judgment, so Christ was sacrificed once to take away the sins of many people; and he will appear a second time, not to bear sin, but to bring salvation to those who are waiting for him. Hebrews 9:27& 28

Take a Moment….
  ….to give someone flowers.

_____
_____
_____
_____
_____
_____

October 21
Yon will again have compassion on us; you will tread our sins underfoot and hurl all our iniquities into the depths of the sea. Micah 7:19

_____
_____
_____
_____
_____
_____

October 22

And if the Spirit of him who raised Jesus from the dead is living in you, he who raised Christ from the dead will also give life to your mortal bodies through his Spirit, who lives in you. Romans 8:11

October 23

The sun will no more be your light by day, nor will the brightness of the moon shine on you, for the Lord will be your everlasting light, and your God will be your glory. Isaiah 60:1

October 24
No temptation has seized you except what is common to man. And God is faithful; he will not let you to be tempted beyond what you can bear. But when you are tempted, he will also provide a way out so that you can stand up under it. 1 Corinthians 10:13

_____
_____
_____
_____
_____

October 25
Praise be to the God and Father of our Lord Jesus Christ! In his great mercy he has given us new birth into a living hope through the resurrection of Jesus Christ from the dead, 2 Peter 1:3

_____
_____
_____
_____
_____
_____

October 26
But Samuel replied: Does the Lord delight in burnt offerings and sacrifices as much as in obeying the voice of the Lord? To obey is better than sacrifice.
1 Samuel 15:22

October 27
For he has rescued us from the dominion of darkness and brought us into the kingdom of the Son he loves,
Colossians 1:13

Take a Moment….
…to pray for your family.

October 28
For the grace of God that brings salvation has appeared to all men. It teaches us to say "No" to ungodliness and worldly passions, and to live self-controlled, upright and godly lives in this present age. Titus 2:11& 12

October 29
"Never will I leave you; never will I forsake you"
Hebrews 13:5

October 30
When you pass through the waters, I will be with you; and when you pass through the rivers, they will not sweep over you. When you walk through the fire, you will not be burned; the flames will not set you ablaze.
Isaiah 43:2

October 31
Now we know that if the earthy tent we live in is destroyed, we have a building from God, an eternal house in heaven, not built by human hands. 2 Corinthians 5:1

November

Wake each morning
Knowing that God is with you
In every moment of each day
And, that whenever joy
Touches your life
God smiles because He
Gave it to you
Each sorrow
That comes is one
That He will
Help you to carry

November 1
"if my people, who are called by my name, will humble themselves and pray and seek my face and turn from their wicked ways, then will I hear from heaven and will forgive their sin and will heal their land".
2 Chronicles 7:14

November 2
….and, surely I am with you always, to the very end of the age. Matthew 28:20

November 3

For physical training is of some value, but godliness has value for all things, holding promise for both the present life and the life to come. 1 Timothy 4:8

_____
_____
_____
_____
_____

Take a Moment………
…..to tell someone why you appreciate them.

_____
_____
_____
_____
_____

November 4
For his anger lasts only a moment, but his favor lasts a lifetime; weeping may stay for the night, but rejoicing comes in the morning. Psalm 30:5

_____
_____
_____
_____
_____
_____

November 5
Therefore he is able to save completely those who come to God through him, because he always lives to intercede for them. Hebrews 7:25

_____
_____
_____
_____
_____
_____

November 6
Wealth and honor come from you; you are the ruler over all things. In your hands are strength and power to exalt and give strength to all. 1 Chronicles 29:12

_____
_____
_____
_____
_____
_____

November 7
No one who is born of God will continue to sin, because God's seed remains in them; they cannot go on sinning, because they have born of God. 1 John 3:9

_____
_____
_____
_____
_____

November 8
Ask and it will be given to you; seek and you will find; knock and the door will be opened to you. Matthew 7:7

November 9
All scripture is God-breathed and is useful for teaching, rebuking, correcting and training in righteousness, so that the man of God may be thoroughly equipped for every good work. 2 Timothy 3:16& 17

November 10
I have been crucified with Christ and I no longer live, but Christ lives in me. Galatians 2:20

Take a Moment......
....to ask God for direction.

November 11
You may ask me for anything in my name, and I will do it. John 14:14

_____
_____
_____
_____
_____
_____

November 12
The Lord is good to those whose hope is in him, to the one who seeks him. Lamentations 3:25

_____
_____
_____
_____
_____
_____

November 13
And the peace of God, which transcends all understanding, will guard your hearts and minds in Christ Jesus. Philippians 4:7

November 14
Your faithfulness continues through all generations; you established the earth, and it endures. Psalm 119:90

Quiet Moments…..

I have been prompted today to be grateful instead of taking what I have for granted. I am so thankful for all the years that my family has been safe and secure. We think our families belong to us. They don't. I am thankful for the convenience of a telephone (my phone didn't work for a few days recently) that my car works (even though its 12 years old) and that I have a roof over my head. I have food to eat and clothes to wear. I am grateful to God for His blessings even when I don't notice that it is He who is my provider. At times, I tend to concentrate on what I do not have instead of seeing how much I am given every single day. The Israelites were saved from slavery by God. But, they complained every time their situation became difficult. I am guilty too.

Sometimes, complaining seems justified and it's easier than gratitude.

Lord, make me ever thankful for the cup I have been given whether full or empty.

November 15
Because of the increase of wickedness, the love of most will grow cold, but he who stands firm to the end will be saved. Matthew 24:12 & 13

November 16
God is not unjust; he will not forget your work and the love you have shown him as you have helped his people and continue to help them. Hebrews 6:10

November 17
Thanks be to God for his indescribable gift!
2 Corinthians 9:15

Take a Moment….
….to read an extra chapter in your bible.

November 18
We were therefore buried with him through baptism into death in order that, just as Christ was raised from the dead through the glory of the Father, we too may live a new life. Romans 6:4

November 19
"Don't be afraid." the prophet answered, "Those who are with us are more than those who are with them."
2 Kings 6:16

November 20
For the Lord God is a sun and shield; the Lord bestows favor and honor; no good thing does he withhold from those whose walk is blameless. Psalm 84:11

November 21
It is God who arms me with strength and makes my way perfect. 2 Samuel 22:33

November 22
But thanks be to God, who always leads us in triumphal procession in Christ, and through us spreads everywhere the fragrance of the knowledge of him.
 2 Corinthians 2:14

November 23
I have told you these things, so that in me you may have peace. In this world you will have trouble. But take heart! I have overcome the world. John 16:33

November 24
For it is by grace you have been saved, through faith – and this not from yourselves, it is the gift of God – not by works, so that no one can boast. Ephesians 2:8& 9

_____
_____
_____
_____
_____
_____

Take a Moment….
….to have a cup of cocoa, tea, or coffee and relax.

_____
_____
_____
_____
_____
_____

November 25
"Bring the whole tithe into the storehouse, that there may be food in my house. Test me in this," says the Lord Almighty, 'and see if I will not throw open the floodgates of heaven and pour out so much blessing that you will not have room enough for it". Malachi 3:10

November 26
Here is a trustworthy saying: if we died with him, we will also live with Him. 2 Timothy 2:11

November 27
For the word of God is living and active. Sharper than any double-edged sword, it penetrates even to dividing soul and spirit, joints and marrow; it judges the thoughts and attitudes of the heart. Hebrews 4:12

_____
_____
_____
_____
_____
_____
_____

November 28
Therefore, since we also are surrounded by such a great cloud of witnesses, let us through off everything that hinders and the sin that so easily entangles, and let us run with perseverance the race marked out for us.
Hebrews 12:1

_____
_____
_____
_____
_____
_____
_____

November 29
I lift up my eyes to the hills- where does my help come from? My help comes from the Lord, the Maker of heaven and earth. Psalm 121:1

November 30
Your word, O Lord, is eternal; it stands firm in the heavens. Psalm 119:89

December

The love that radiates from one person

To another is God's smile reaching from heaven to earth

It touches hearts, warms the soul, and

Causes another ray of joy to

Spring forth to yet another person

December 1
He replied, "Blessed rather are those who hear the word of God and obey it." Luke 11:28

Take a Moment…….
…..to send out Christmas greetings.

December 2

And the prayer offered in faith will make the sick person well; the Lord will raise him up. If he has sinned he will be forgiven. James 5:15

December 3

Let us then approach the throne of grace with confidence, so that we may receive mercy and find grace to help us in our time of need. Hebrews 4:16

December 4
Forgive and act; deal with each man according to all he does, since you know his heart (for you alone know the hearts of all men.) 1 Kings 8:39

December 5
"Every word of God is flawless; he is a shield to those who take refuge in him." Proverbs 30:5

December 6
For the Son of Man is going to come in his Father's glory with his angels, and then he will reward each person according to what he has done. Matthew 16:27

_____
_____
_____
_____
_____
_____

December 7
So we fix our eyes not on what is seen, but on what is unseen For what is seen is temporary, but what is unseen is eternal. 2 Corinthians 4:18

_____
_____
_____
_____
_____
_____

December 8

But because of his great love for us, God, who is rich in mercy, made us alive with Christ even when we were dead in transgressions – it is by grace you have been saved. Ephesians 2:4& 5

Praise

Take a Moment.......
…..to sing Christmas carols.

December 9
But remember the Lord your God, for it is he who gives you the ability to produce wealth, and so confirms his covenant, which he swore to your forefathers, as it is today. Deuteronomy 8:18

_____
_____
_____
_____
_____
_____

December 10
My dear children, I write this to you so that you will not sin. But if anybody does sin, we have one who speaks to the Father in our defense -Jesus Christ the righteous one. 1 John 2:1

_____
_____
_____
_____
_____
_____

December 11
But if we walk in the light, as he is in the light, we have fellowship with one another, and the blood of Jesus, his Son, purifies us from all sin. 1 John 1:7

_____
_____
_____
_____
_____

December 12
But I tell you the truth: It is for your good that I am going away. Unless I go away, the Counselor will not come to you; but if I go, I will send Him to you.
John 16:7

_____
_____
_____
_____
_____

December 13
He who did not spare his own Son, but gave him up for us all- how will he not also, along with him, graciously give us all things? Romans 8:32

December 14
The Lord your God is with you, he is mighty to save. He will take great delight in you, he will quiet you with his love, he will rejoice over you with singing.
Zephaniah 3:17

Quiet Moments…..

A hand that reaches out for mine
Words unspoken, yet understood
The sound of a thunderstorm, the smell of rain
A crisp autumn morning
Leaves blowing in the wind
Fresh fallen snow
Evergreens silhouetted against a star-filled night
Wading in an effervescent stream and splashing water
Sitting on green grass with the warm sun upon my face
Sand betweens my toes
Hillsides dotted with wildflowers
The sound of crickets on a summer evening
Voices raised in worship
My senses are constantly being filled with the wonder of your love, Lord.

December 15

For you know the grace of our Lord Jesus Christ, that though he was rich, yet for your sakes he became poor, so that you through his poverty might become rich.
2 Corinthians 8:9

Take a Moment……
….to attend a Christmas program.

December 16
The word became flesh and made his dwelling among us.
We have seen his glory, the glory of the One and Only,
who came from the Father, full of grace and truth.
 John 1:14

December 17
May he strengthen your hearts so that you will be
blameless and holy in the presence of our God and Father
when our Lord Jesus Christ comes with all His holy ones.
1 Thessalonians 3:13

December 18
Those who trust in the Lord are like Mount Zion, which cannot be shaken but endures forever. Psalm 125:1

December 19
Those who know your name will trust in you, for you, Lord, have never forsaken those who seek you. Psalm 9:10

December 20
He gives strength to the weary and increases the power of the weak. Isaiah 40:29

_____
_____
_____
_____
_____

December 21
For in the day of trouble he will keep me safe in his dwelling; he will hide me in the shelter of his tabernacle and set me high upon a rock. Psalm 27:5

_____
_____
_____
_____
_____

December 22

The Lord will rescue me from every evil attack and will bring me safely to his heavenly kingdom. 2 Timothy 4:18

Merry Christmas

Take a Moment…..

…to tell someone about what Jesus has done for you.

December 23
Then you will call, and the Lord will answer; you will cry for help, and he will say: Here am I. Isaiah 58:9

December 24
I will lie down and sleep in peace, for you alone, O Lord, make me dwell in safety. Psalm 4:8

December 25
For to us a child is born, to us a son is given, and the government will be upon his shoulders. Isaiah 9:6

_____

_____

_____

_____

December 26
And there were shepherds living out in the fields nearby, keeping watch over their flocks at night. An angel of the Lord appeared to them, and the glory of the Lord shone around them, and they were terrified. But the angel said to them, "Do not be afraid. I bring you good news of great joy that will be for all the people. Today in the town of David a Savior has been born to you; he is Christ the Lord". Luke 2:8-12

_____

_____

_____

_____

December 27
I have told you this so that my joy might remain in you and that your joy may be complete. John 15:11

December 28
Commit to the Lord whatever you do, and your plans will succeed. Proverbs 16:3

December 29
But Thanks be to God! He gives us the victory through our Lord Jesus Christ. 1 Corinthians 15:57

Take a Moment…..
……to pray for wisdom, guidance, and blessings in the coming year.

December 30
Delight yourself in the Lord and he will give you the desires of your heart. Psalm 34:4

December 31
My sheep listen to my voice; I know them, and they follow me. I give them eternal life, and they shall never perish; no one can snatch them out of my hand.
John 10:27

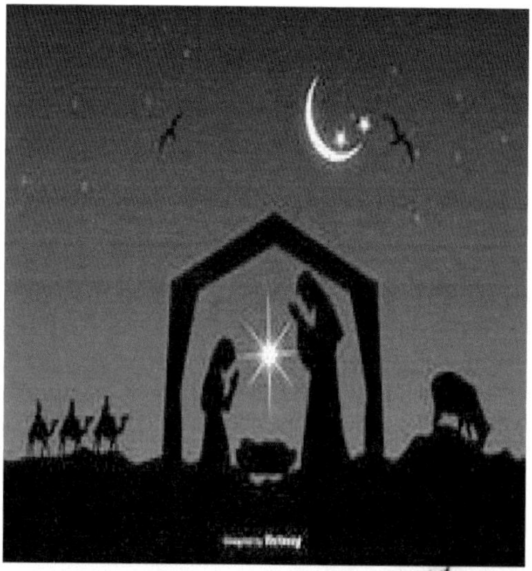

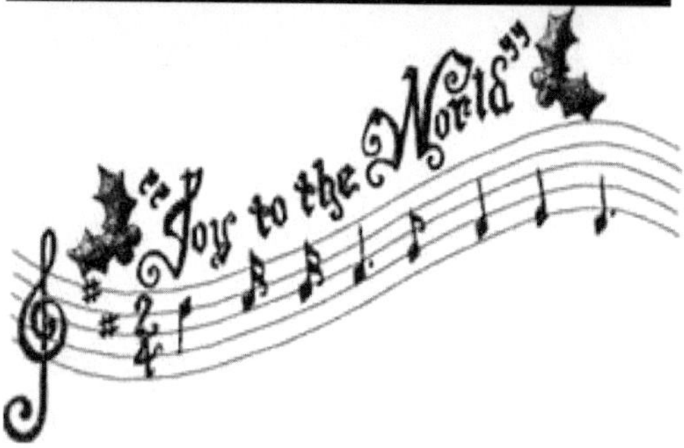
"Joy to the World"

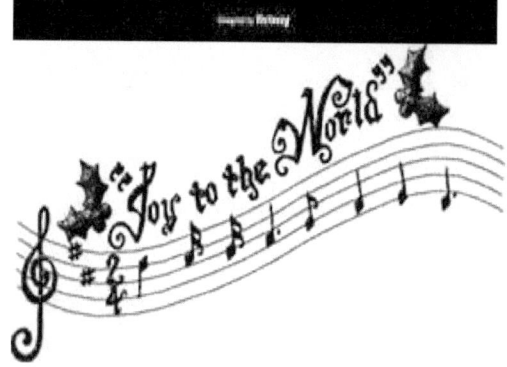